WEAPONS
OF THE
CIVIL WAR

BY MATT DOEDEN

CAPSTONE PRESS
a capstone imprint

Blazers Books are published by Capstone Press,
1710 Roe Crest Drive, North Mankato, Minnesota 56003
www.mycapstone.com

Library of Congress Cataloging-in-Publication Data
Names: Doeden, Matt, author.
Title: Weapons of the Civil War / by Matt Doeden.
Description: North Mankato, Minnesota: Capstone Press, [2017] | Series: Blazers. Weapons of
  War | Includes bibliographical references and index.
Identifiers: ISBN 978-1-5157-7909-4 (library hardcover) | ISBN 978-1-5157-7920-9 (eBook PDF)
Subjects: LCSH: Survival—Juvenile literature.
Classification: E491 .D64 2018
LC record available at https://lccn.loc.gov/2016055804

Editorial Credits
Bradley Cole, editor; Kyle Grenz, designer; Jo Miller, media researcher;
Gene Bentdahl, production specialist

Photo Credits
Alamy: INTERFOTO, 13 (both); Bridgeman Images: Civil War Archive, 16 (top middle), Don Troiani,
8, 11, 16 (bottom and bottom middle), 17 (right), 25 (bottom), Private Collection, 15; Getty Images:
Corbis Historical, 19, MPI, 5, Stock Montage, 28; iStockphoto: LUGO, 25 (middle left), Mark Kostich,
cover (top right), Teacherdad48, cover (bottom); Library of Congress: Prints and Photographs
Division, 9, 24 (bottom right and top), 25 (top left); Newscom: akg-images, 20, Everett Collection, 6,
Heritage Images/Ann Ronan Picture Library, 25 (top right), KRT/George Barnard, 27; North Wind
Picture Archives, 10, Nancy Carter, 24 (bottom left); Shutterstock: Everett Historical, 23, Kletr, cover
(right), Robert B. Miller, cover (left and middle), Russell Shively, cover (top left), SAJE, cover (top);
Wikimedia: Hmaag (talk), 16 (top), National Park Service, 17 (top)

Design Elements: Shutterstock: autsawin uttisin, Bennyartist, Dinga, donatas1205, mamanamsal,
Milan M, Nikola Markovic 81, Paladin12, Sergey Andrianov

Printed and bound in China
PO004598

TABLE OF CONTENTS

A Nation Divided

The boom of **cannons** fills the air. Soldiers fall to the ground during a bloody U.S. Civil War (1861–1865) battle.

cannon—a large gun that fires large explosive shells

FACT

During the Civil War, the Northern states were called the Union. The Southern states were called the Confederacy.

FACT

The first battle of the Civil War was the battle of Fort Sumter. Not one person died in that battle.

The Civil War was a dark time in U.S. history. The Northern and Southern states had different views about **slavery** and states' rights. The two sides fought each other with powerful weapons.

slavery—the owning other people; slaves are forced to work without pay

the attack on Fort Sumter by Confederate forces in 1861

Rifles, Revolvers, and Blades

Civil War soldiers carried **rifles**. These long guns had to be reloaded after every shot. Northern soldiers carried the 1861 Springfield. It had good **range** but was slow to load.

≫ 1861 SPRINGFIELD RIFLE

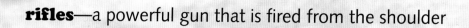

rifles—a powerful gun that is fired from the shoulder

range—the distance that a bullet can travel

a Union soldier with his rifle and bayonet

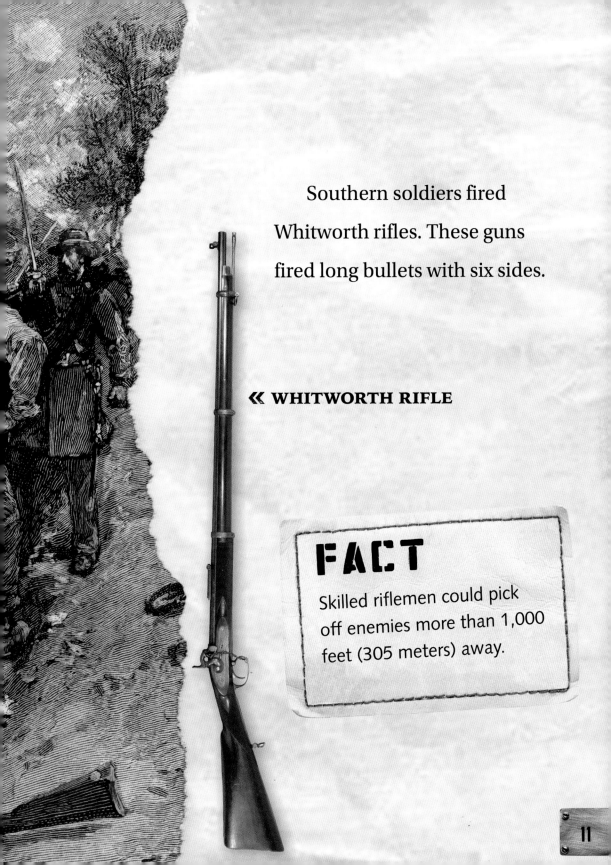

Southern soldiers fired
Whitworth rifles. These guns
fired long bullets with six sides.

« **WHITWORTH RIFLE**

FACT

Skilled riflemen could pick
off enemies more than 1,000
feet (305 meters) away.

Some soldiers also used small guns called revolvers. Northern soldiers shot Colt revolvers. Southern soldiers used LaMat revolvers. LaMats fired nine shots before they needed to be reloaded.

FACT

Soldiers on horseback used revolvers so they could easily ride and shoot at the same time.

COLT REVOLVER

LAMAT REVOLVER

13

Blades worked well in hand-to-hand fighting. **Bayonets** fit onto the ends of rifles. Soldiers on horseback attacked enemies with **sabers**.

bayonet—a blade attached to the end of a rifle

saber—a sword with a slightly curved blade

Union soldiers

SMALL ARMS

« COLT REVOLVER

⌃ SPENCER REPEATING RIFLE

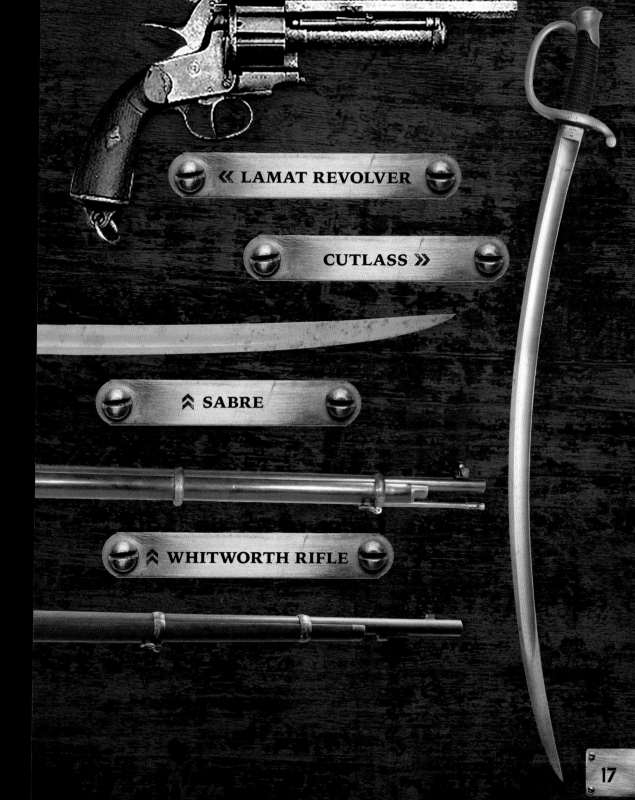

« LAMAT REVOLVER

CUTLASS »

⌃ SABRE

⌃ WHITWORTH RIFLE

The Big Guns

Large weapons were called **artillery**. They did the most damage. A cannon shot could kill 10 soldiers or more.

artillery—cannons and other large guns

a cannon at Fort Gaines, Alabama

a Gatling machine gun

The Gatling gun was one of the first machine guns. Soldiers turned a handle to fire the gun. It had six barrels. Each barrel fired 100 bullets per minute.

FACT

Richard Gatling invented the Gatling gun. He improved the gun over several years. A later model had 10 barrels.

Both sides fired the Howitzer. This cannon could hit targets 1 mile (1.6 kilometers) away. Soldiers also threw **grenades** and launched **mortar** shells at enemies.

grenade—a small bomb that can be thrown

mortar—a short cannon that shoots small explosive shells

Confederate soldiers with a Howitzer cannon

23

LARGER WEAPONS

⌃ **12-POUND CANNON**

⌃ **PARROT CANNON**

⌄ **32-POUND CANNON**

13-INCH MORTAR

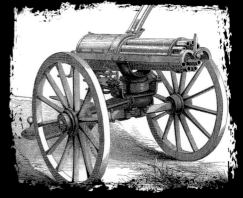

GATLING GUN

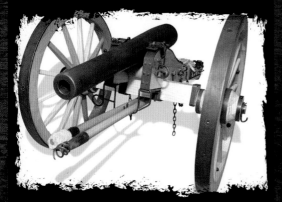

ORDNANCE RIFLE

HAND GRENADE

Line of Defense

Both armies tried to slow enemy travel. They built barriers called **chevaux-de-frise** (shuh-voh-duh-FREEZ) across main roads. These barriers were made of angled wooden spikes.

cheval-de-frise—a log with a pointed tip placed into rivers and roads to block enemy forces; the plural form is chevaux-de-frise

a Confederate chevaux-de-frise in Atlanta, Georgia

Soldiers had little defense against powerful cannons and rifles. Before the Civil War ended, 620,000 Americans had died.

FACT

About 50,000 soldiers ended up killed, wounded, or missing in the battle of Gettysburg in 1863.

Glossary

artillery (ar-TI-luhr-ee)—cannons and other large guns used during battles

bayonet (BAY-uh-net)—a long metal blade attached to the end of a musket or rifle

cannon (KAN-uhn)—a large gun that fires large explosive shells

cheval-de-frise (shuh-val-duh-FREEZ)—a log with a pointed tip placed into rivers and roads to block enemy forces; the plural form is chevaux-de-frise

grenade (gruh-NAYD)—a small bomb that can be thrown or launched

mortar (MOR-tur)—a short cannon that shoots small, explosive shells

range (RAYNJ)—the maximum distance ammunition can travel to reach its target

rifle (RYE-fuhl)—a powerful gun that is fired from the shoulder

saber (SAY-bur)—a sword with a curved blade and one cutting edge

slavery (SLAY-vur-ee)—the owning of other people; slaves are forced to work without pay

Read More

Delmar, Pete. *Vehicles of the Civil War*. War Vehicles. North Mankato, Minn.: Capstone Press, 2014.

Lanser, Amanda. *The Civil War by the Numbers*. America at War by the Numbers. North Mankato, Minn.: Capstone Press, 2016.

Mattern, Joanne. *Technology During the Civil War*. Military Technologies. Minneapolis: Abdo, 2016.

Internet Sites

FactHound offers a safe, fun way to find Internet sites related to this book. All of the sites on FactHound have been researched by our staff.

Here's all you do:

Visit *www.facthound.com*

Type in this code: 9781515779094

Check out projects, games and lots more at **www.capstonekids.com**

Index